THE
MAGNIFICENT
BOOK
OF
ANIMALS

THE MAGNIFICENT BOOK OF ANIMALS

ILLUSTRATED BY
Val Walerczuk

WRITTEN BY
Tom Jackson

First published in the UK by
Weldon Owen
King's Road Publishing
The Plaza
535 King's Road
London SW10 0SZ
www.weldonowen.co.uk
www.bonnierpublishing.com

Created by:
Author: Tom Jackson
Illustrator: Val Walerczuk
Senior Editor: Lydia Halliday
Designer: Rod Teasdale
Consultant: Joanne Dorning
Publisher: Donna Gregory

Printed in China

10 9 8 7 6 5

ISBN: 978-1-78342-201-2

Introduction

From the icy Arctic to the hot African savanna, animals live in every corner of the world. They can be found swinging from trees, snuggling underground, or scaling the tallest mountain peaks. And some of the largest, most amazing creatures on Earth are mammals.

Mammals are warm-blooded, give birth to live offspring, feed milk to their young, and are covered in hair. This may sound familiar – humans are mammals too! In fact, there are more than 5,000 different types of mammals living all over the world. They can be cute and cuddly, smart and stealthy, or fierce and ferocious.

The Magnificent Book of Animals showcases some of the most fascinating mammals on the planet through oversized, stunning illustrations. Amazing facts accompany every animal, describing the behaviour that makes each one unique. The illustrations and fascinating facts bring the animals vividly to life and provide a sneak peek into what you could expect if you ever met these animals in the wild.

Fact file

Lives: North America

Habitat: Mountain forest

Length: 1.7–2.8 m (5 ft 5 in–9 ft 2 in)

Weight: 130–360 kg (290–790 lb)

Lifespan: 25–30 years

Diet: Fish, deer, and fruits

Learn about the playful chimpanzee, the sleepy koala, the lumbering hippopotamus, and more magnificent animals inside!

Contents

African elephant

Loxodonta africana

- An elephant's tusks are its two front teeth. They can be as long as a man is tall.
- A baby elephant eats a little of its mother's poo. It's a way of making its tummy healthy!
- Elephants talk to each other using very deep rumbles that travel through the ground as vibrations.
- Elephants are the only animals in the world with four knees.
- An elephant's trunk has 100,000 different muscles.

Fact file

Lives: Africa

Habitat: Forests and grasslands

Height: 3.2–4 m (10–13 ft)

Weight: 1,700–6,100 kg (3,748–13,448 lb)

Lifespan: 60–70 years

Diet: Roots, leaves, grasses, fruit, and bark

- An elephant's teeth are so huge that there is only room for four teeth at a time in its mouth. It grows new ones as each tooth gradually wears and falls out.
- A trunk is strong enough to knock down a tree, but also sensitive enough to pick up a twig.
- An elephant's wrinkly skin traps droplets of moisture which helps to keep it cool in the hot sun.

Panda bear

Ailuropoda melanoleuca

- The giant panda has a sixth "finger" on its forepaws, where a wrist bone sticks out to hold bamboo shoots.
- A panda has to eat all the time. It can only sleep for 4 hours at a time before it has to wake up to eat some more.
- Pandas peel off the outside of the bamboo with their teeth and then eat the softer insides.
- Giant pandas like to be alone. If two bears meet each other they will growl and hit each other until one runs away.
- A panda goes to the toilet 40 times a day!
- Male pandas do handstands so that they can scent mark tree trunks with glands on their rear ends.
- Newborn panda cubs are 900 times smaller than a female adult. That makes them the smallest babies of any mammal apart from marsupials.

Fact file

Lives: China
Habitat: Bamboo forest
Length: 1.2–1.8 m (4–6 ft)
Weight: 100–150 kg (220–331 lb)
Lifespan: 15–20 years
Diet: Bamboo

Reindeer

Rangifer tarandus

 Male reindeer are called bulls, while females are called cows.

 Reindeer are the only type of deer where both the male and female grow antlers.

 The reindeer that live in North America are known as caribou.

 In winter, reindeer grow hair out of their feet to keep them warm in the snow.

 Reindeer are the only mammals that can see in ultraviolet light.

 In winter, a reindeer has nothing to eat but bark, twigs, and their favourite food, lichen.

 In summer, reindeer have a short brown coat; in winter the coat is grey and much shaggier.

 A bull reindeer has antlers in summer; a cow has antlers during the winter.

Fact file

Lives: Arctic region

Habitat: Tundra and forests

Length: 1.5–2.3 m (5–7 ft 6 in)

Weight: 60–318 kg (130–700 lb)

Lifespan: 10–15 years

Diet: Leaves, grass, twigs, mushrooms, and lichen

Grey wolf

Canis lupus

- Despite all the fairy stories, wolves very rarely attack humans.
- A group of wolves is called a pack. The pack works together to hunt down large animals.
- Before humans inhabited all continents, the wolf was the most widely spread mammal in the world.
- A wolf cub's eyes are blue but they turn yellow as it gets older.
- The howl of a wolf can be heard up to 16 km (10 miles) away.

Fact file

Lives: North America, Asia, eastern and northern Europe

Habitat: Tundra and forest

Length: 1.5 m (5 ft)

Weight: 36–54 kg (180–20 lb)

Lifespan: 8–13 years

Diet: Rabbits, deer, rodents

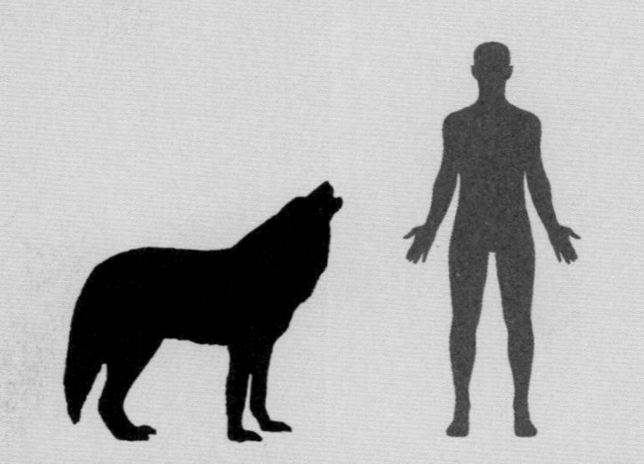

- All pet dogs have descended from tame wolves that started to live alongside people about 20,000 years ago.
- A wolf can eat 9 kg (20 lb) in one meal. That's the same as a human eating 100 hamburgers.

Mandrill

Mandrillus sphinx

- A male mandrill's lips are often stuck in a snarl so they show off its long teeth.
- When the male is angry, the colours on his face become brighter and he thumps the ground.
- The mandrill is the largest monkey in the world. The males are too big to climb very high into trees.
- Mandrills live in huge groups called hordes. The largest horde ever counted contained 1,200 mandrills.

Fact file

Lives: Central Africa

Habitat: Lowland forest

Length: 75–95 cm (2 ft 6 in–4 ft)

Weight: 10–35 kg (22–77 lb)

Lifespan: 20–30 years

Diet: Fruit, nuts, roots, and small animals

- Mandrills save food for later by stuffing it into pouches in their cheeks.
- As well as a blue and red face and yellow beard, male mandrills have a purple bottom.

Flying fox

Pteropus vampyrus

- Flying foxes are the largest fruit bats in the world. They are ten times bigger than the smallest species.
- The wingspan of a flying fox is 1.5 m (5 ft). Stretched out, the bat would cover most of your bed.
- Flying foxes eat fruit and flowers. They hang from trees and pull food towards them with claws on their wings.
- Flying foxes find food using their large eyes and sensitive noses.
- Bats sleep upside down in caves and trees. Their feet never get tired when gripping a branch.
- Flying foxes dunk their bodies in water and then fly back to the roost to lick the water off.

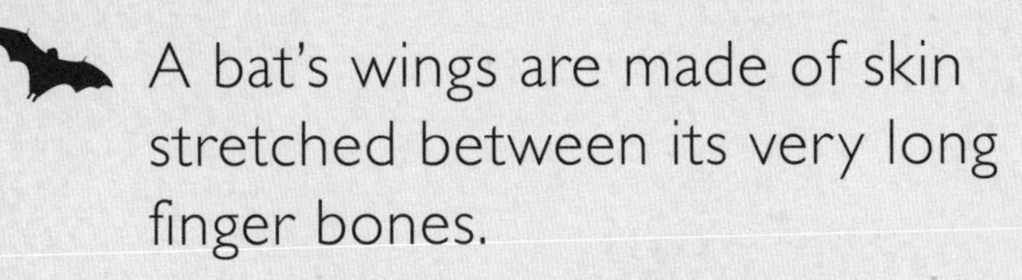

A bat's wings are made of skin stretched between its very long finger bones.

Fact file

Lives: Southeast Asia

Habitat: Rainforest

Length: 18–22 cm (7–9 in)

Weight: 0.65–1.2 kg (1 lb 4 oz–2 lb 6 oz)

Lifespan: 15 years

Diet: Flowers and fruit

Snow leopard

Panthera uncia

- Snow leopards are the only big cat that cannot roar.
- This mountain leopard holds the animal long jump record. It can leap 15 metres (49 feet) – the length of a bus.
- The leopard wraps its bushy tail around its feet to keep warm in the snow.
- The snow leopard's smoky grey camouflage is so good it is known as the ghost cat.
- This cat can climb two thirds of the way up Mount Everest, making it the highest hunting mammal in the world.
- The leopard's spots get paler in winter so it can hide better among the snow-covered rocks.
- A female lines her den with scraps of her own fur to make it cosy for her cubs.

Fact file

Lives: Central Asia

Habitat: Mountains

Length: 0.9–1.2 m (3–4 ft)

Weight: 35–55 kg (77–121 lb)

Lifespan: 9–10 years

Diet: Sheep, goats, deer, and smaller mammals like marmots

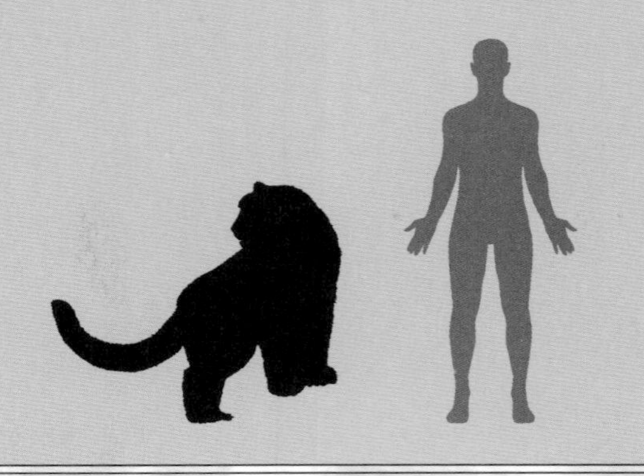

Przewalski's horse

Equus przewalskii

- Przewalski's horse is the oldest breed of horse still living today.
- Przewalski's horses were first discovered in Mongolia, a huge area of grasslands in Central Asia.
- Przewalski's horses have never been tamed, which means they are the last truly wild horses in existence.
- Horses can smell water from many kilometres away and gallop off for a drink.
- A horse's eyes face sideways. They can look at things all around them but cannot see what is directly in front.

Fact file

Lives: Worldwide today, but originally China, Mongolia, and parts of Russia and Europe

Habitat: Grasslands, semi-desert

Height: 1.2–1.4 m (4 ft–4 ft 6 in)

Weight: 200–340 kg (440–750 lb)

Lifespan: 20 years

Diet: Grass and leaves

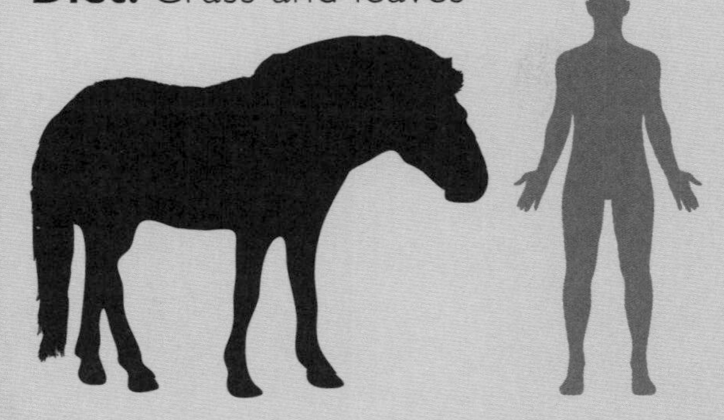

- Ponies are not young horses but small ones. A young horse is called a filly or colt.
- A herd of horses is led by one large male, called the stallion. The rest of the herd are females, or mares.

Red kangaroo

Macropus rufus

- A female kangaroo is called a jill; a male is known as a jack; a baby is a joey.
- The red kangaroo is the largest living marsupial.
- A newborn joey weighs just 0.75 grams and has no back legs. It crawls through its mother's fur to her pouch.
- The red kangaroo can bounce 10 m (33 ft) in one go.
- When moving slowly, the kangaroo balances on its thick tail, using it as a fifth leg.
- A kangaroo fights like a boxer, jumping forward and punching its attacker with its front paws.
- A joey stays in the pouch for six months before it is strong enough to start exploring outside.

Fact file

Lives: Australia

Habitat: Grassland

Height: 0.8–1.6 m (2 ft 7 in–5 ft 4 in)

Weight: 20–90 kg (44–180 lb)

Lifespan: 6–8 years

Diet: Grass and shrubs

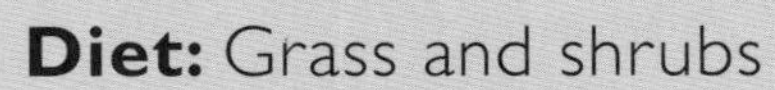

Lion

Panthera leo

- Lions are the only cats that live in family groups.
- Only a male lion has a mane. It is a sign of how healthy it is – the darker the better.
- A lion's tummy is very stretchy so it can eat a quarter of its body weight in one meal.
- Lions are the only cats to have a tassel on their tail. They raise it to show where they are in long grass.

Fact file

Lives: Africa (and one forest in India)

Habitat: Grassland

Length: 1.5–2 m (5 ft–6 ft 5 in)

Weight: 120–250 kg (265–550 lb)

Lifespan: 10–14 years

Diet: Antelopes, zebras

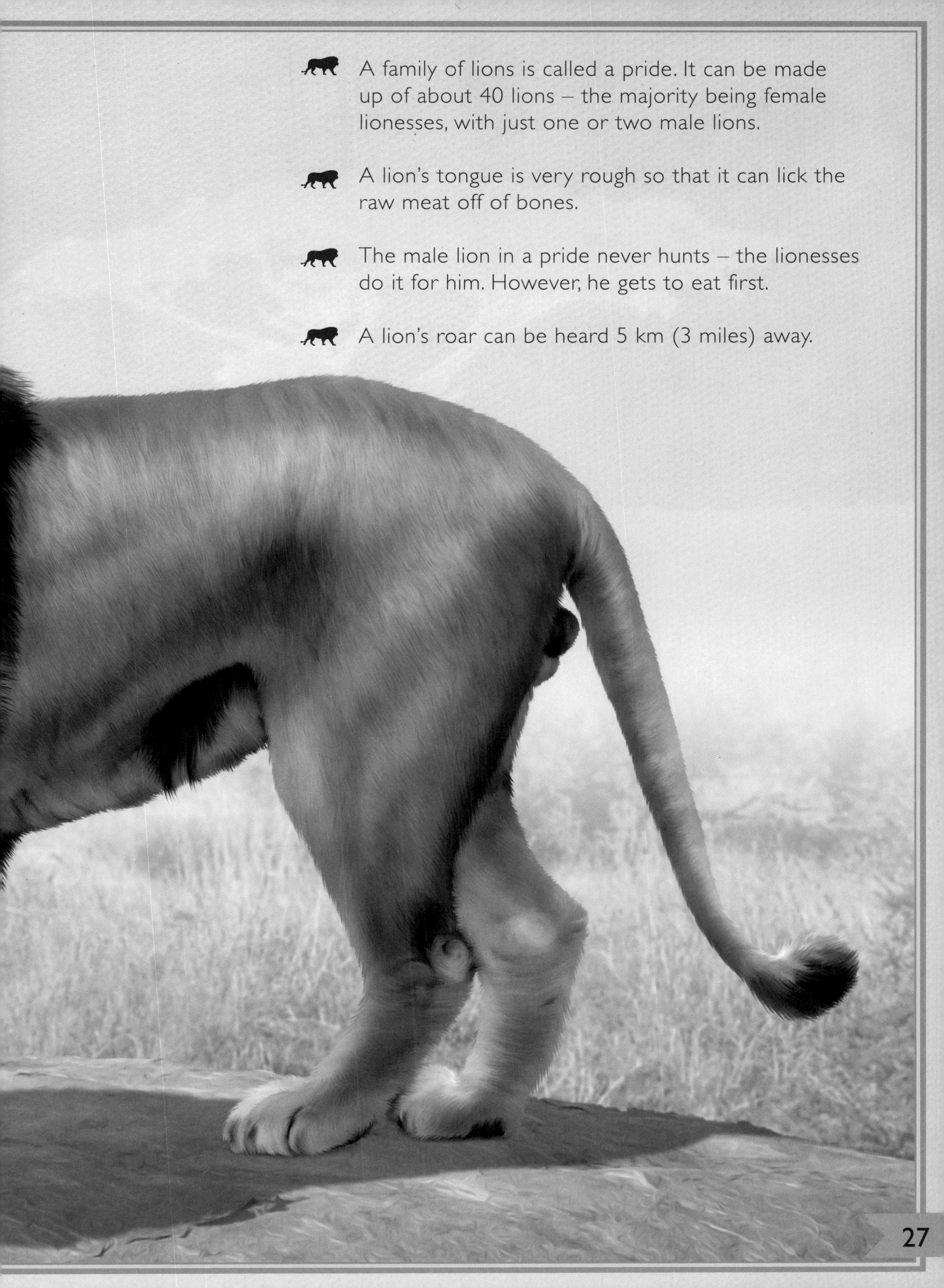

- A family of lions is called a pride. It can be made up of about 40 lions – the majority being female lionesses, with just one or two male lions.
- A lion's tongue is very rough so that it can lick the raw meat off of bones.
- The male lion in a pride never hunts – the lionesses do it for him. However, he gets to eat first.
- A lion's roar can be heard 5 km (3 miles) away.

Polar bear

Ursus maritimus

- A polar bear's hairs are not white but see-through. The light reflecting off them makes them look white.
- Polar bears spend the summer at sea – walking on the frozen ocean or swimming up to 100 km (60 miles) to find food.
- Polar bears do not sleep or hibernate. Only pregnant females dig a den into the snow and live off of their fat reserves for the period of their pregnancy.
- Polar bears have 10 cm (4 in) of fat under the skin. This keeps them warm and is a food store for when they cannot hunt.

Fact file

Lives: Arctic Ocean

Habitat: Ice and tundra

Length: 2–2.5 m (6 ft 6 in–8 ft 2 in)

Weight: 150–500 kg (330–1,100 lb)

Lifespan: 15–18 years

Diet: Seals, fish, deer, and berries

- Polar bears feed on seals. They can smell their prey through the ice that covers the ocean.

- Polar bear cubs are born inside the winter snow den, usually in late January.

- The hairs on a polar bear are hollow and full of air. This makes them good at keeping the bear warm.

Dromedary

Camelus dromedarius

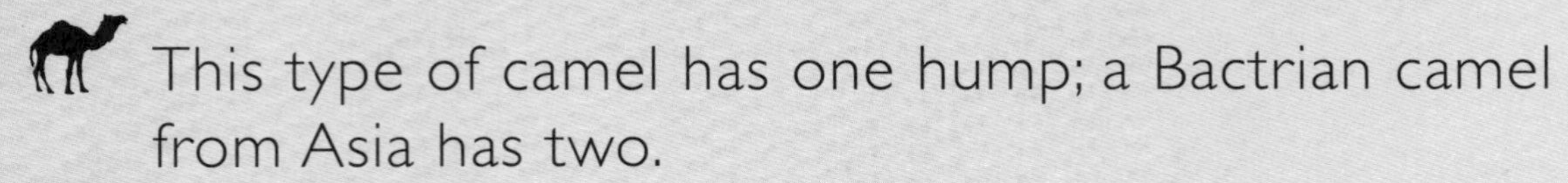

- This type of camel has one hump; a Bactrian camel from Asia has two.
- As long as it has water, a dromedary can go for months without eating.
- The hump is a store of fat, not water, which keeps the camel alive as it walks across empty deserts.
- In the 1800s, dromedaries were taken to Australia. Many of them escaped and now live in huge wild herds.
- A dromedary can close its nostrils during a sandstorm.

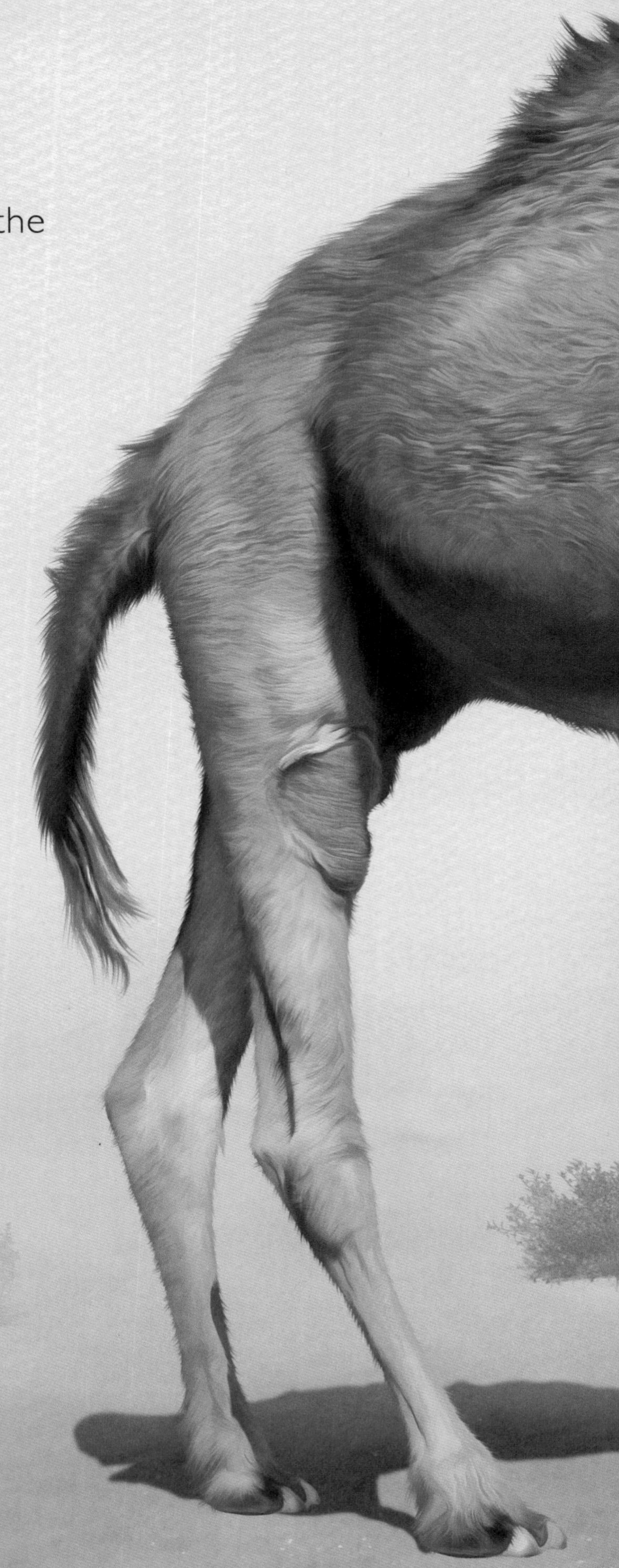

Fact file

Lives: Africa, Middle East

Habitat: Desert

Length: 3 m (10 ft)

Weight: 300–690 kg (661–1,521 lb)

Lifespan: 40–50 years

Diet: Plants

- When frightened, camels spit some of their juices at attackers. Yuk!
- A baby dromedary has no hump, just a tassel of hairs where one will grow later.

Orang-utan

Pongo pygmaeus

- A baby orang-utan lives with its mother for eight years. That is the longest childhood in the animal kingdom.
- When it rains, an orang-utan uses a large leaf as an umbrella.
- Orang-utan means "old man of the forest" in the Malay language.
- An orang-utan's arms are much longer than its legs. This makes them great swingers.
- Many male orang-utans have a wide, round pad on their cheeks. Females do not have these.
- Orang-utans eat 300 different types of fruit. They feed in the morning and evening and snooze during the middle of the day.

Fact file

Lives: Sumatra and Borneo
Habitat: Rainforest
Length: 1.25–1.5 m (4–5 ft)
Weight: 30–90 kg (66–200 lb)
Lifespan: 35–45 years
Diet: Fruits, leaves, and eggs

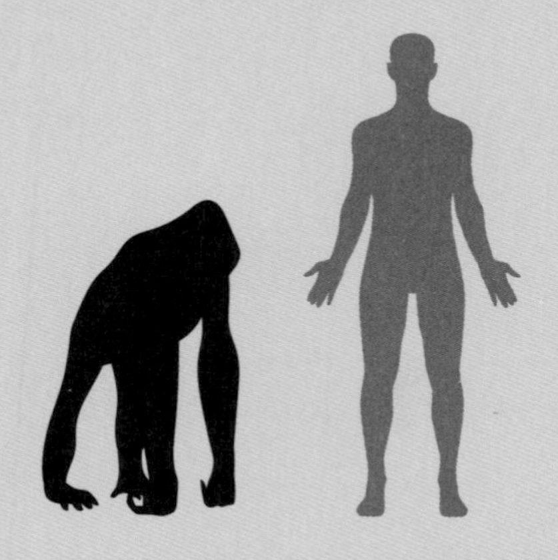

Every night, orang-utans build a fresh nest out of folded branches so they can sleep high in the trees.

Okapi

Okapia johnstoni

- An okapi's tongue is so long that the animal can lick its eyes and ears clean.
- Okapi calves keep track of their mothers in dense forest by looking for stripes on her rump.
- An okapi can listen to two sounds at once by twisting its ears to point in different directions.
- Only the male okapi has horns. They point backwards so they do not get tangled in the forest branches.
- An okapi's hooves produce a smelly jelly that leaves a trail of scent wherever it goes.

Fact file

Lives: Central Africa
Habitat: Rainforest
Length: 1.9–2.5 m (6 ft 1 in–8 ft)
Weight: 200–350 kg (44–770 lb)
Lifespan: 20–30 years
Diet: Leaves, twigs, and fruit

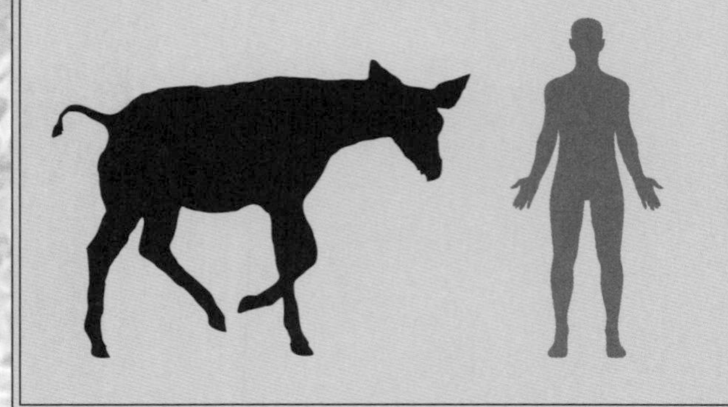

- Okapis communicate with sounds so deep that predators (and humans) cannot hear them.
- The red-brown coat of an okapi makes them very difficult to see among the tree trunks and branches of the shady forest.

Grizzly bear

Ursus arctos

- The grizzly bears of Kodiak Island in Alaska are the largest land predators in the world.
- A grizzly bear is a type of brown bear named after the streaky colours on its fur. Each dark hair has a pale tip.
- Newborn bear cubs hum as they drink their mother's milk. The sound makes her produce more milk.
- Grizzlies have a hump between their shoulders. This contains the huge muscles that move the front legs.

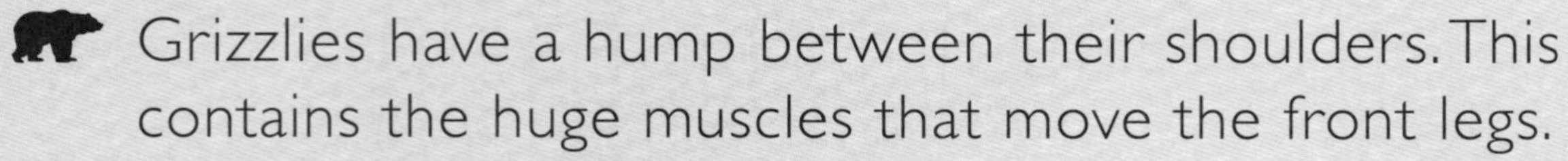

Fact file

Lives: North America

Habitat: Mountain forest

Length: 1.7–2.8 m (5 ft 5 in–9 ft 2 in)

Weight: 130–360 kg (290–790 lb)

Lifespan: 25–30 years

Diet: Fish, deer, and fruits

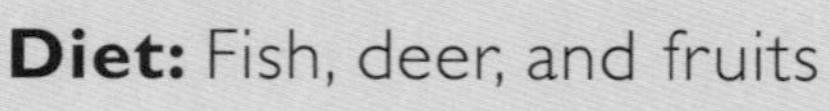

- Brown bears cover their leftover food with moss and grass. Chemicals in the moss stop the food from rotting.
- A brown bear loses a third of its weight as it sleeps through the winter.
- During its long winter sleep, the bear does not go to the toilet for six months!

Chimpanzee

Pan troglodytes

- Chimpanzees are more closely related to humans than any other animal.
- Chimps eat particular "medicine" leaves when they feel unwell.
- Chimps communicate with facial expressions: a big grin means a chimp is scared, not happy.
- A chimp chews the end of a stick to make it soft and uses that to soak up drinking water from hard to reach spots.
- Chimps make friends by kissing each other and grooming bugs out of each other's fur.

Fact file

Lives: Central Africa

Habitat: Tropical forest

Length: 1.3–1.6 m (4–5 ft)

Weight: 32–60 kg (70–130 lb)

Lifespan: 45 years

Diet: Plants, insects, and meat

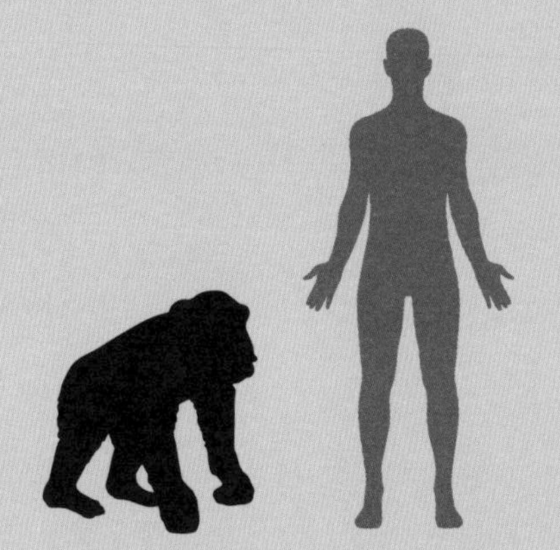

- Chimps hate deep water and are bad swimmers.
- Unlike other apes, chimps work as a team to hunt for animals, such as monkeys and small deer.

Arctic fox

Alopex lagopus

- The Arctic fox changes the colour of its coat. In winter it is white, in summer it turns grey-brown.
- Arctic fox dens are hundreds of years old because the animals cannot dig new ones in the frozen ground.
- The fox's ears can hear lemmings, its favourite food, scurrying around under deep snow – and it then pounces right on to them.

Fact file

Lives: Arctic

Habitat: Tundra

Length: 70–100 cm (2 ft 4 in–3 ft 3 in)

Weight: 3–8 kg (6 lb 6 oz–17 lb 6 oz)

Lifespan: 3–6 years

Diet: Rabbits, voles, fish, berries, and mushrooms

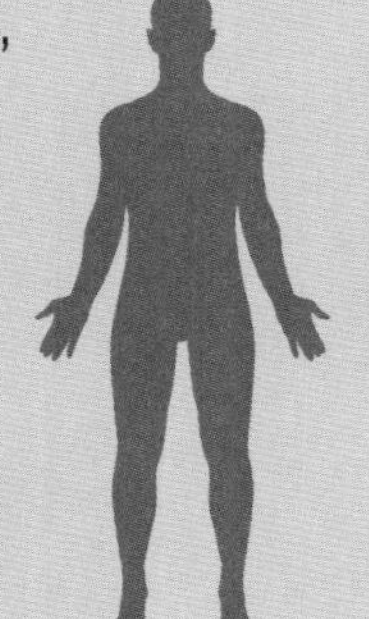

- Arctic foxes can withstand a temperature of -50°C (-58°F). Any colder than that, and it stays in its den until it warms up.
- The Arctic fox has very small ears compared to other foxes. This stops them from getting frostbite in the winter.
- The Arctic fox is the only land mammal native to Iceland.
- If they cannot find their own food, an Arctic fox will follow a polar bear and eat its leftovers.

Tapir

Tapirus indicus

- The tapir is a relative of horses and rhinos.
- The tapir's body is narrow at the front and wide at the back, which helps it to push through thick undergrowth.
- Their trunk-like noses are flexible and can wrap around branches to strip off leaves.
- Tapirs whistle to each other through the dense undergrowth of their forest habitat.
- There are five types of tapir: Malayan tapirs lives in Southeast Asia. All other types of tapir live in the jungles of Central and South America.

Fact file

Lives: Southeast Asia, South America, and Central America

Habitat: Forests

Length: 1.8–2.5 m (5 ft 9 in–8 ft 3 in)

Weight: 250–375 kg (551–827 lb)

Lifespan: 30 years

Diet: Leaves, fruits, and berries

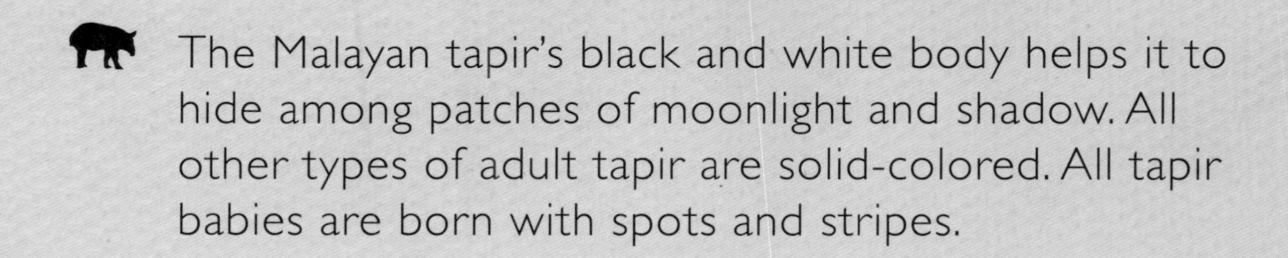

- The Malayan tapir's black and white body helps it to hide among patches of moonlight and shadow. All other types of adult tapir are solid-colored. All tapir babies are born with spots and stripes.

- According to a Thai legend, the tapir was made from the leftovers of other animals.

Tiger

Panthera tigris

- Tigers mark their territory with claw marks scraped into trees and even rocks.
- Unlike most cats, tigers like water. They swim across rivers and lie in wait for prey in the shallow waters.
- A tiger kills one or two animals each week. It buries the leftovers to eat later.
- A tiger can kill an animal that weighs four times more than itself.

Fact file

Lives: Southern and Eastern Asia

Habitat: Forests and swamps

Length: 2–3.3 m (6 ft 6 in–10 ft 8 in)

Weight: 65–306 kg (143–675 lb)

Lifespan: 10–12 years

Diet: Deer, cattle, and pigs

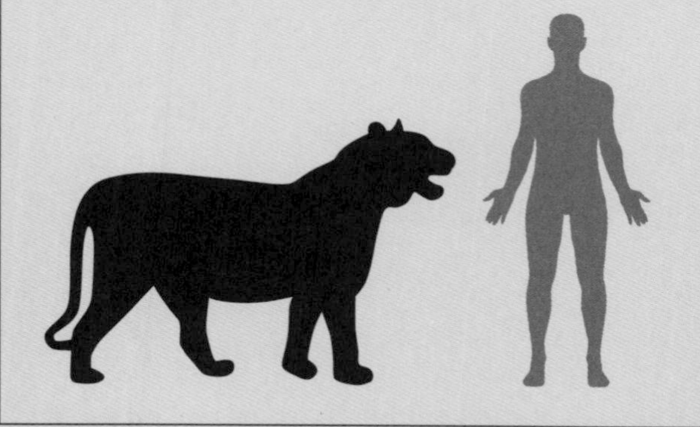

- The largest tigers live in Siberia. They have fewer dark stripes so they blend in with the snow better.
- Tigers kill their prey by biting their victims' necks so that they cannot breathe.
- A tiger controls a huge territory – about the size of the island of Hawaii.

Warthog

Phacochoerus africanus

- Warthogs go into their burrows backwards so their tusks are always facing towards the entrance ready for an attack.
- When warthogs are running from danger, they raise their tails to warn the others.
- The warts on a warthog's face are there to protect their eyes during battles.
- A warthog is related to a pig. It uses its pig-like snout to sniff out buried food.
- Warthogs kneel down to get closer to the ground when they are eating grass.

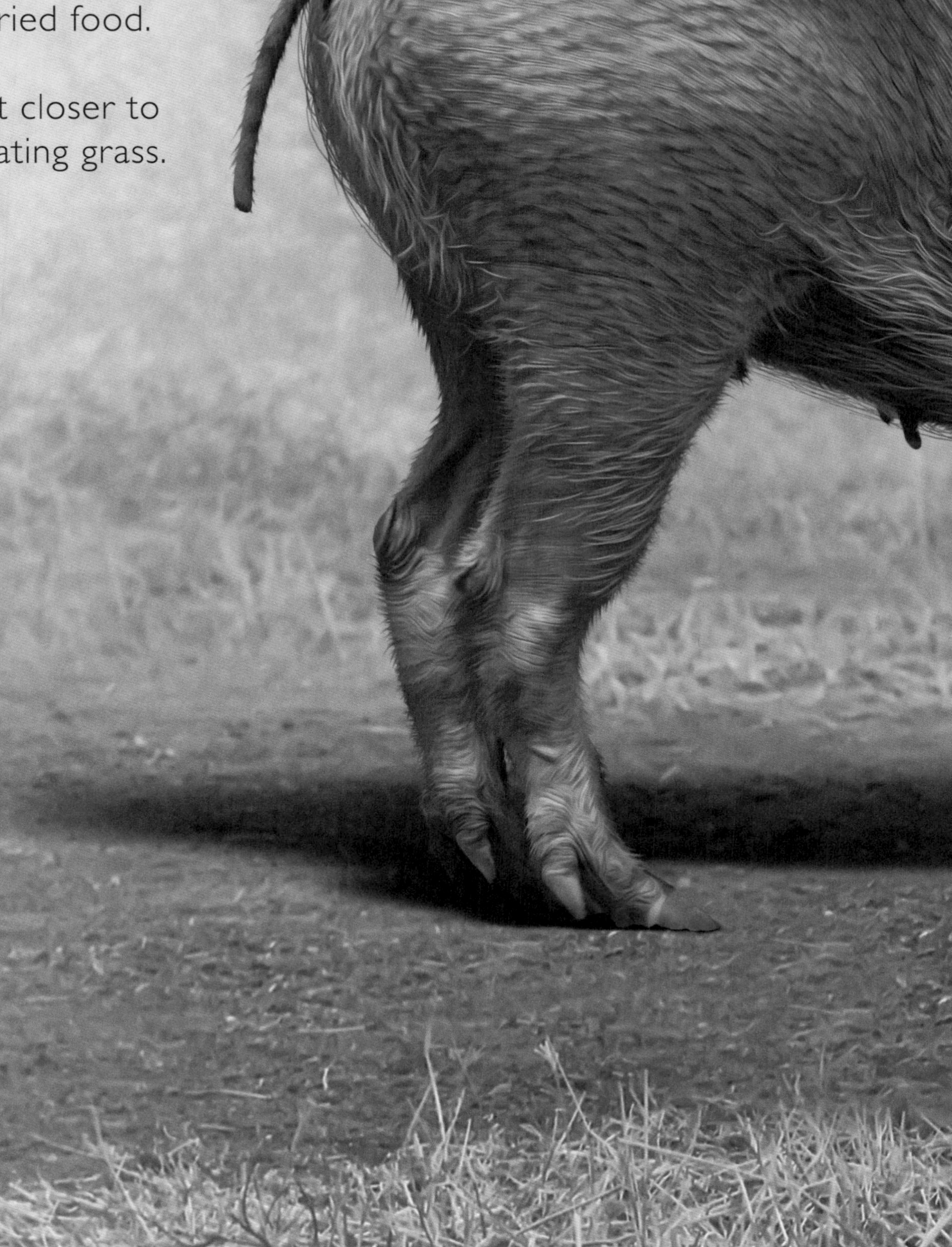

Fact file

Lives: Africa
Habitat: Grassland and woodland
Length: 0.9–1.5 m (3–5 ft)
Weight: 50–150 kg (110–330 lb)
Lifespan: 12–15 years
Diet: Grass, roots, and berries

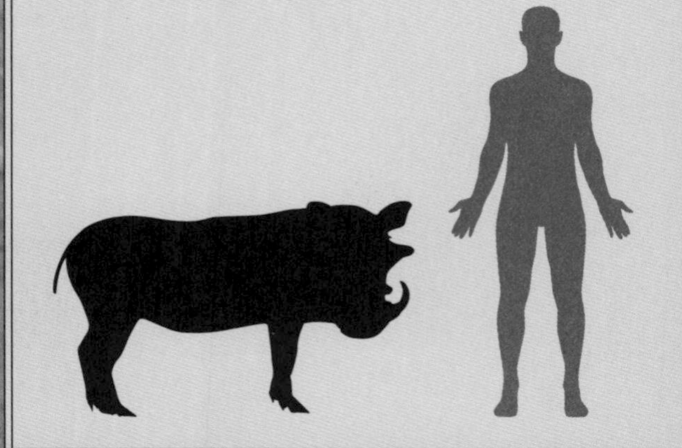

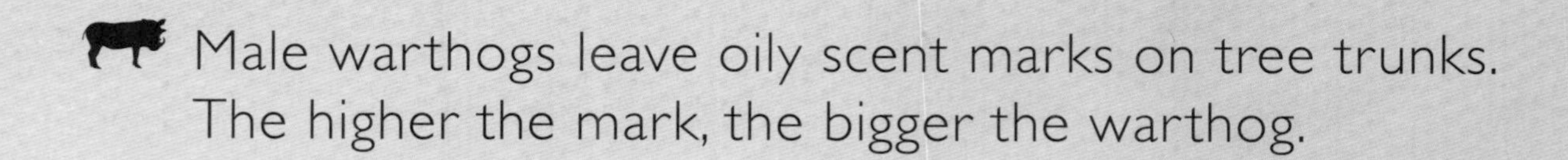

Male warthogs leave oily scent marks on tree trunks. The higher the mark, the bigger the warthog.

Warthogs have four tusks. The lower pair are the sharpest and are used for fighting predators.

Beaver

Castor fiber

- A beaver's front teeth never stop growing. They are worn away by chewing wood.
- A beaver can cover its eyes with a clear eyelid. These work like goggles and help the beaver to see underwater.
- Beavers dam rivers with mud and logs to make the water much deeper. This protects them against predators, and enables them to keep food and building materials afloat.
- Beavers build lodges by making a pile of mud and stones and then burrowing out a den.
- The outside of their muddy lodge freezes solid in winter making it impossible for any predator to dig into it.

Fact file

Lives: Europe, Asia, and North America

Habitat: Rivers and lakes

Length: 80–100 cm (2 ft 6 in–3 ft 3 in)

Weight: 11–30 kg (24–66 lb)

Lifespan: 7–8 years

Diet: Grasses and wood pulp

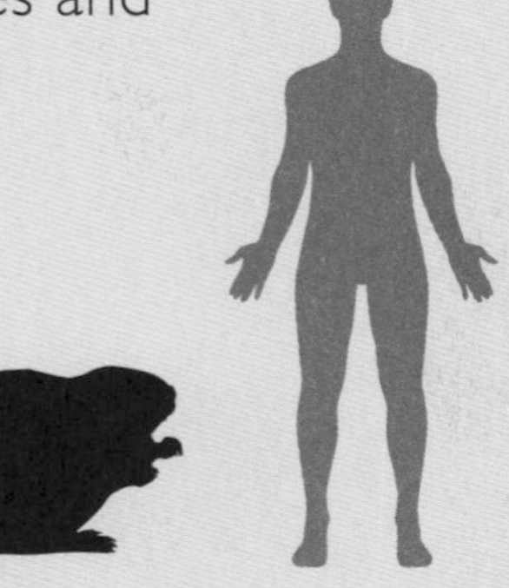

- Inside, the lodge has two rooms. The entrance chamber is used for drying off, and the inner den is kept dry for sleeping.
- Beavers use their tails for steering in water – and as a comfy seat when sitting on the bank.

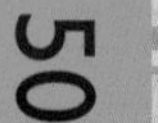

Giraffe

Giraffa camelopardalis

- The giraffe is the tallest animal in the world. Its head would reach a second storey window.
- Giraffes have seven neck bones – the same number as you.
- The tongue of a giraffe is blue. It is 50 cm (20 in) long and is very flexible.
- Male giraffes fight by knocking their necks together.
- Giraffes have one of the shortest sleep requirements of any mammal, needing only 10 minutes to 2 hours within a 24 hour period.
- A giraffe is born with two skin-covered horns. They are flat on the head to begin with but stand up as the giraffe gets older.

- Female giraffes give birth standing up. The baby falls 2 m (6 ft) to the ground.
- A giraffe's heart beats twice as hard and twice as fast as a human's to pump blood up its long neck.

Fact file

Lives: Africa

Habitat: Woodland and savannah

Length: 3.8–4.7 m (12 ft 5 in–15 ft 5 in)

Weight: 680–1,400 kg (1,499–3,086 lb)

Lifespan: 25 years

Diet: Leaves

Koala

Phascolarctos cinereus

- Koalas sleep for 20 hours each day.
- Koalas keep their fur clean by combing it with a long claw on their front paw.
- Koalas smell of eucalyptus which comes from the oily leaves they eat.
- Fossils show that 100,000 years ago, there was a type of koala the size of a cow.
- A koala's small brain is floating in fluid, which cushions it if it falls out of a tree and lands on its head.
- Koalas have to eat a mouthful of soil every now and then. The germs in the soil help it to digest its leaves.
- A baby koala lives in its mother's pouch. The opening of the pouch faces backwards.

Fact file

Lives: Eastern Australia
Habitat: Woodlands and forests
Length: 64–82 cm (2 ft–2 ft 7 in)
Weight: 4–15 kg (8.8–33 lb)
Lifespan: 13–18 years
Diet: Eucalyptus leaves

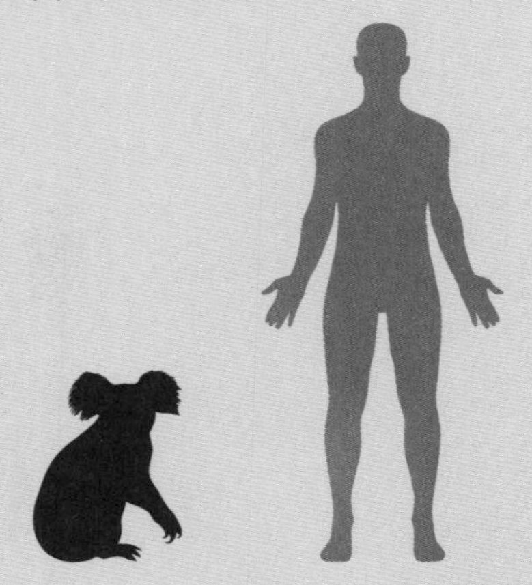

Zebra

Equus quagga

 Zebras can sleep standing up, but one herd member always stands guard.

 Every zebra has a unique pattern of black (or brown) stripes on their white fur.

 Zebras have black skin under the white fur. Nobody knows the reason why they have stripes!

 The stripes make a herd of zebras blend together, and lions find it difficult to follow one target in the crowd.

Fact file

Lives: Africa

Habitat: Savannah and woodlands

Length: 2.5 m (8 ft 3 in)

Weight: 250–300 kg (551–661 lb)

Lifespan: 40 years

Diet: Grasses

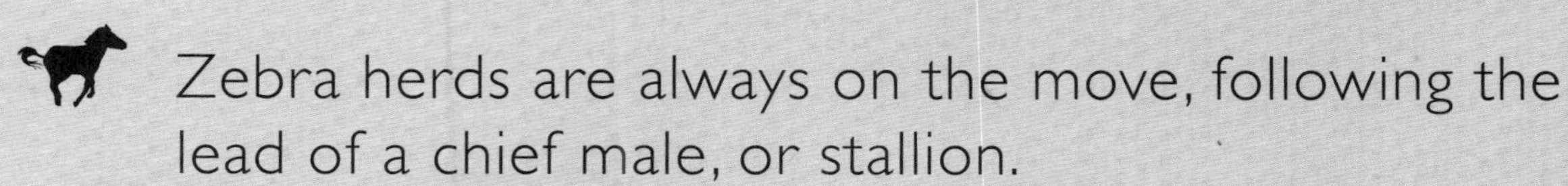

- Zebra herds are always on the move, following the lead of a chief male, or stallion.

- Zebras dig into dry riverbeds with their hooves to make small watering holes.

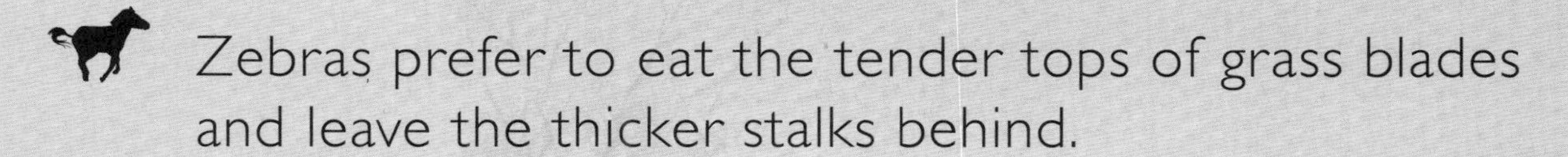

- Zebras prefer to eat the tender tops of grass blades and leave the thicker stalks behind.

Sloth

Bradypus pygmaeus

- There are six sloth species, all of which live in the tropical rainforests of Central and South America. Some have two toes, some have three.
- Sloths move very slowly along branches so eagles and other predators do not see them.
- Their long shaggy fur gets very dirty and goes green from all the mould and algae living in it.
- A sloth can do almost anything hanging upside down – except go to the toilet. It moves to the ground to do that.
- The hair of most mammals grows down their bodies, but because a sloth is upside-down, its hair grows up the body!

 A sloth is born in the trees and must grab its mother's long hair to stop itself falling to the ground.

 It takes a whole month for a meal of leaves to pass through a sloth's gut.

Fact file

Lives: Central America, South America

Habitat: Rainforest

Length: 50 cm (1 ft 7 in)

Weight: 2.5–3.5 kg (5 lb 5 oz–7 lb 7 oz)

Lifespan: 20–30 years

Diet: Leaves and fruit

Bison

Bison bison bison

- In the nineteenth century, hunters killed at least 50 million bison to clear the land for cattle farms.
- This animal is sometimes called a buffalo but it is only a distant relative of the real buffaloes that live in Africa and Asia.
- Their winter coat is so thick and well insulated that snow can cover their backs without melting.
- In spring, bison look very untidy as their thick winter coats fall away.
- Bison have bad eyesight, but they can smell another animal 3 km (2 miles) away.

Fact file

Lives: North America

Habitat: Woodlands and prairie

Length: 2–3.5 m (6 ft 5 in–11 ft 5 in)

Weight: 360–1,000 kg (794–2,205 lb)

Lifespan: 15–20 years

Diet: Grass

- A healthy adult bison has no enemies. Hunters like wolves and mountain lions only attack the young and the very old.
- Bison are good swimmers. Their bodies float in the water.

Hippopotamus

Hippopotamus amphibius

- The word hippopotamus means "horse of the river".
- A hippo's skin produces red liquid. This works like sunscreen to protect against sunburn.
- A hippo often yawns, but not because it is tired. It is showing other hippos how big its teeth are.
- Hippos use water to stay cool during the day. At night they come onto the bank to eat grass.
- A hippo uses its tail to fling poo around. This helps to spread its smell so other animals know where it lives.

Fact file

Lives: Africa

Habitat: Rivers and lakes

Length: 3 m (9 ft 9 in)

Weight: 600–2,000 kg (1,323–4,409 lb)

Lifespan: 40 years

Diet: Grass

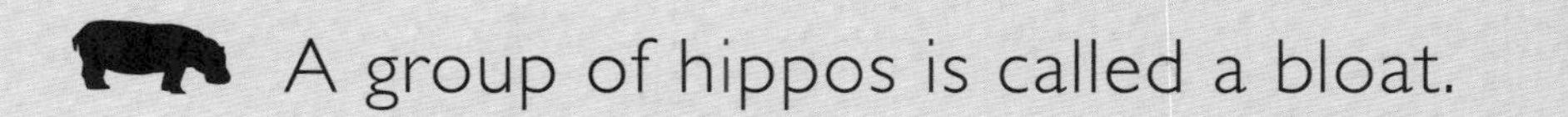

- A group of hippos is called a bloat.
- A hippo's skin is about 6 cm (2.5 in) thick!
- A hippo can close its ears and nostrils when it dives underwater.

Gorilla

Gorilla gorilla

- The leader of a gorilla troop is the largest, strongest silverback. He has grey hair on his back.
- Gorillas eat a large breakfast of leaves and fruit, and then take a midday nap!
- Gorillas scare attackers away by slapping their chests with cupped hands. It makes a loud thumping sound.
- A gorilla troop moves to a new place in the forest everyday to find fresh food.

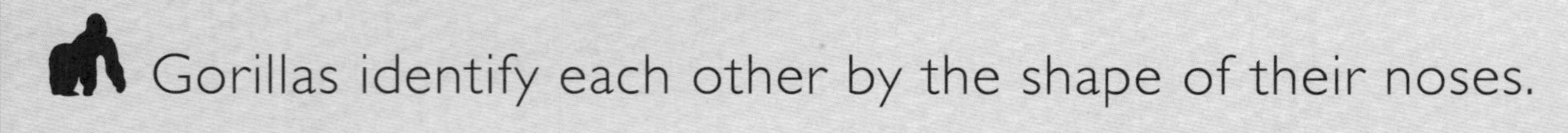

- Gorillas identify each other by the shape of their noses.

Fact file

Lives: Central Africa
Habitat: Lowland tropical forests
Length: 1.5–1.7 m (5 ft–5 ft 6 in)
Weight: 72–170 kg (159–375 lb)
Lifespan: 35–40 years
Diet: Leaves, fruit, and shoots

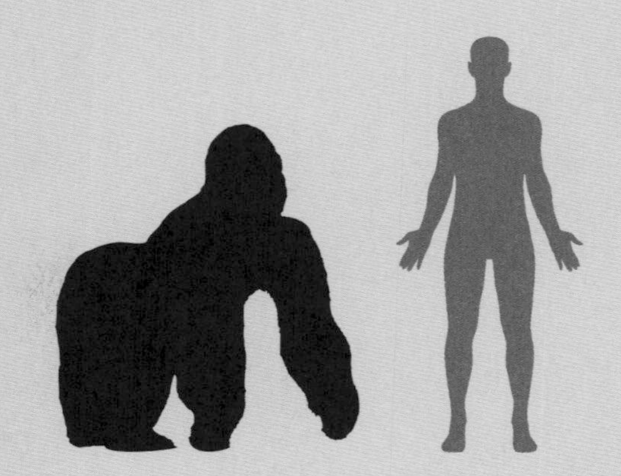

The word gorilla comes from the ancient Greek term for "tribe of hairy women".

Gorillas normally walk on four legs, leaning on the knuckles of their hands.

White rhinoceros

Ceratotherium simum

- A white rhino's skin is grey-brown; the "white" name comes from their wide mouths.
- A rhino's horn is made from the same stuff found in hair, fingernails, and claws.
- An adult rhino keeps its horn sharp by rubbing it against trees.
- The name rhinoceros means "nose horn".

Fact file

Lives: Africa

Habitat: Grassy savannah

Length: 3.6–4.2 m (11 ft 8 in–13 ft 8 in)

Weight: 1,400–2,300 kg (3,086–5,071 lb)

Lifespan: 40–50 years

Diet: Grass

- Male rhinos charge at their enemies at a speed of 65 kmh (40 mph), which is three times as fast as a human can run.
- A rhino's huge head and horns weigh almost 500 kg (1,100 lb), the same as 8 average grown-up humans!
- A rhino may let an oxpecker bird ride on its back. In return the bird keeps the rhino's skin clean.
- Rhinos are very rare because they are hunted for their amazing horns which are incorrectly believed to have medicinal properties.

Wolverine

Gulo gulo

- Wolverines look like hairy dogs but they are actually a giant relative of the weasel.
- Wolverines have very wide feet which work like snowshoes – they do not sink in deep snow.
- Wolverines have long claws which are used as spikes for gripping ice on frozen mountains.
- Baby wolverines, or kits, are born in winter and have white fur to blend in with the snow.

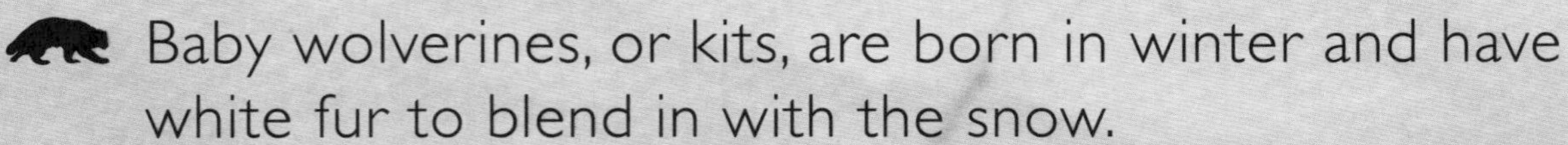

Fact file

Lives: North America, Siberia, and Scandinavia

Habitat: Tundra and forests

Length: 65–105 cm (2 ft–3 ft 5 in)

Weight: 11–18 kg (24–40 lb)

Lifespan: 7–12 years

Diet: Carrion, eggs, rodents, and fruit

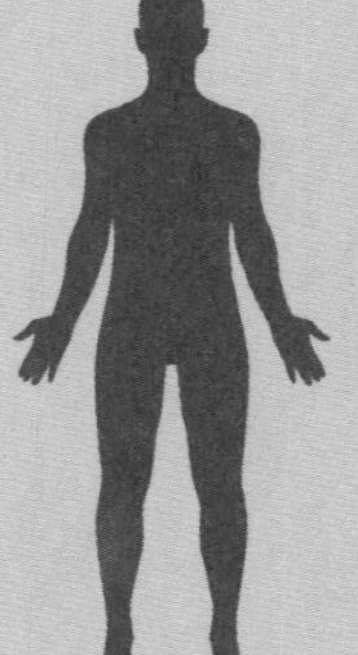

- Wolverines are very fierce. They can even scare grizzly bears away and steal their food.

- If a wolverine cannot finish a meal, it sprays it with a smelly liquid and buries it for later.

- In winter, wolverines use snow like a refrigerator. They cover extra food in snow so it will stay fresh for several weeks.

Ring-tailed lemur

Lemur catta

- This type of lemur fights using smells. Rivals waft smells at each other using their tails.
- Lemurs are related to monkeys. They live only on the island of Madagascar.
- Ring-tailed lemurs are active both at night and during the day – they sleep whenever they want.
- Lemurs are expert climbers, but spend a third of their time sifting through fallen leaves for food.
- The ancestors of lemurs came from Africa and floated over to Madagascar aboard floating logs and branches.

Fact file

Lives: Madagascar

Habitat: Forests and bushland

Length: 39–46 cm
(1 ft 3 in–1 ft 6 in)

Weight: 2.2–3.4 kg
(4 lb 9 oz–7 lb 5 oz)

Lifespan: 16–19 years

Diet: Fruits, leaves, sap, and flowers

Ibex

Capra ibex

- These animals live on steep mountainsides where no other animals can climb.
- The ibex's hoof is in two halves that work like pincers to grip onto the steep rocky ledges.
- A baby ibex, or kid, can run and jump just a few hours after it is born.
- Male ibex have huge curved horns; females have horns too but they are straight and pointed.
- Ibex living in desert areas have shiny coats which reflect the hot sunlight away.

Fact file

Lives: Europe, Asia, and Africa
Habitat: Mountain pastures
Length: 75–170 cm (2 ft 5 in–5 ft 6 in)
Weight: 40–120 kg (88–264 lb)
Lifespan: 10–14 years
Diet: Grass and leaves

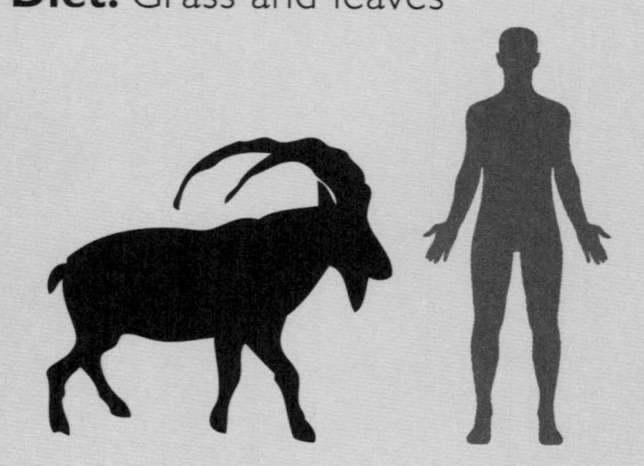

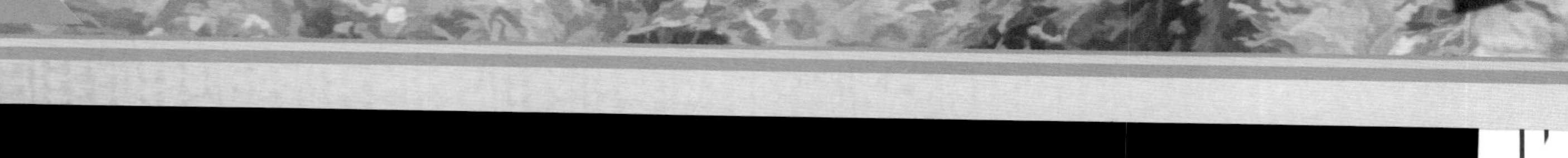

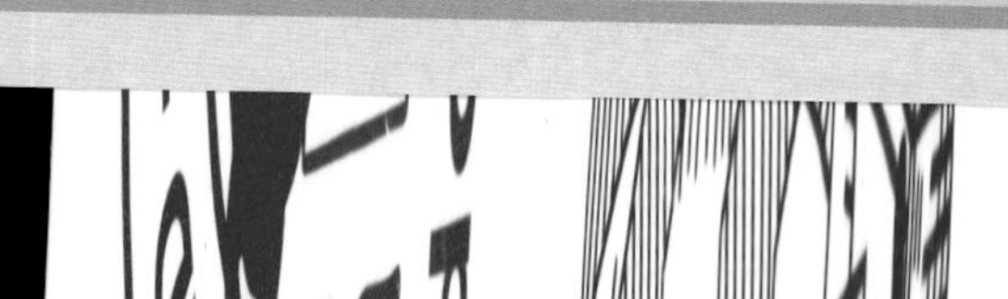

- An ibex can jump nearly 2 m (6 ft 5 in) straight up.
- Ibex lick mountain rocks to get extra salt that is missing from their leafy food.

Leopard

Panthera pardus

- A black panther is a leopard with dark fur. It still has spots but you can't see them very well.
- A leopard's ears are five times more sensitive than a human's.
- Leopards can jump 3 m (9 ft 10 in) into the air. They could leap over a football goal quite easily.
- Leopards are the largest cats that can climb trees. They go up there to sleep.

Fact file

Lives: Africa and southern Asia
Habitat: Forest and grasslands
Length: 1–1.9 m (3 ft 3 in–6 ft 1 in)
Weight: 30–90 kg (66–199 lb)
Lifespan: 12–17 years
Diet: Antelope and deer

- Leopards spot each other by looking for the white spots on the tip of the tail and on the back of each ear.
- A leopard's spotty coat makes it harder for other animals to see their full shape among trees and long grass.
- A leopard points its whiskers forward when it is stalking prey, and folds them back again when sniffing the air.
- A leopard can purr and miaow as well as roar. Its roar is a series of deep, short barks.

Duck-billed platypus

Ornithorhynchus anatinus

- The platypus has a spike or spur on its ankles used in fighting. A male's spur produces venom.
- The platypus is one of just two types of mammal that lay eggs instead of giving birth to their young.
- The duck bill mouth is a sensor which can detect animals buried on the muddy riverbed.
- When scientists first saw a duck-billed platypus specimen, they thought it was several different animals sewn together for a joke!

Fact file

Lives: Eastern Australia

Habitat: Lakes and streams

Length: 30–45 cm (12–18 in)

Weight: 0.5–2 kg (1 lb 1 oz–4 lb 4 oz)

Lifespan: 13 years

Diet: Crustaceans, insects, snails, fish

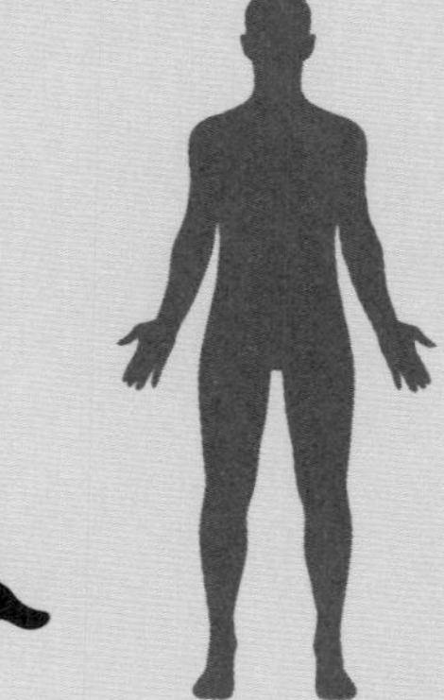

- A platypus dives for less than a minute and has to keep swimming to stay underwater or it would float back to the surface.
- A platypus's flat tail is used as a food store as well as a swimming aid.
- A platypus closes its eyes underwater and relies on its sensitive bill to find its way around.

Striped hyena

Hyaena hyaena

- These animals give out a chuckling call when nervous to warn others to stay away.
- Striped hyenas have one of the strongest bites of any animal. They can crack through a bone with their teeth.
- They look like big dogs or small lions but in fact hyenas are more closely related to the mongoose.
- Striped hyenas can hunt for food, but most of the time they steal the kills of larger animals and eat them.
- When it is ready to fight a hyena raises the hair around its neck. This makes it look bigger and tougher.

Fact file

Lives: Africa

Habitat: Grasslands, woodlands

Length: 86–150 cm (2 ft 9 in–4 ft 11 in)

Weight: 22–55 kg (49–121 lb)

Lifespan: 12 years

Diet: Antelopes, zebras

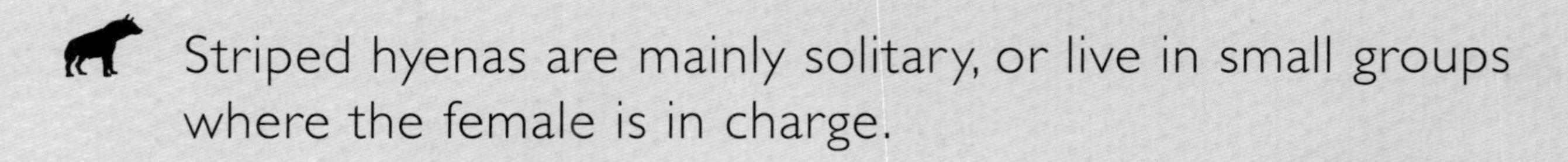

- Striped hyenas are mainly solitary, or live in small groups where the female is in charge.
- In the Serengeti, striped hyenas walk an average of 19 km (12 miles) per night looking for food.

Rondo dwarf bush baby

Galagoides rondoensis

- The Rondo dwarf bush baby lives in one patch of forest in East Africa. It is one of the rarest mammals in the world. Other types of bush babies live in forests across Africa.
- Bush babies pee on their hands so that they leave a scent trail behind as they climb through the forest.
- Bush babies sleep all day and come out to look for food at night.
- Bush babies have very big eyes for seeing in the dark and use their huge ears to pick up the sounds of nearby insects.

- A bush baby has two tongues. A small lower tongue is used for licking its fur clean.
- Another name for the bush baby is galago.
- A bush baby mother carries its baby in her mouth, and pops it on a branch when she feeds.

Fact file

Lives: Africa

Habitat: Rainforest

Length: 12.3–13.7 cm (4–5 in)

Weight: 60 g (2 oz)

Lifespan: 4 years

Diet: Insects, fruit, seeds, flowers, eggs, and tree gums

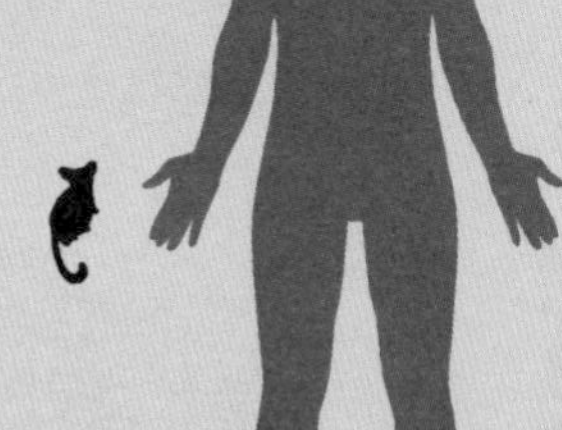

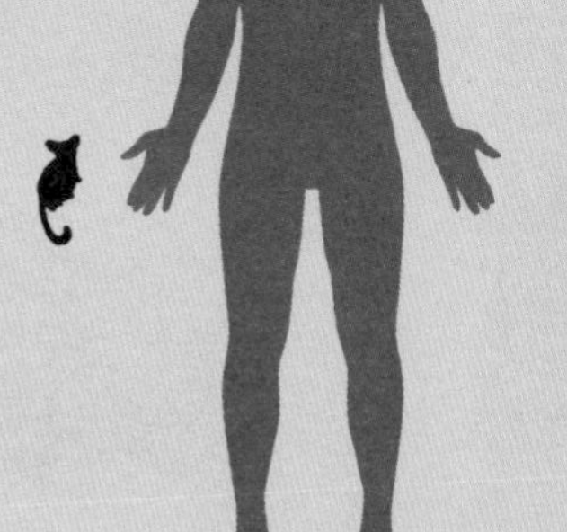

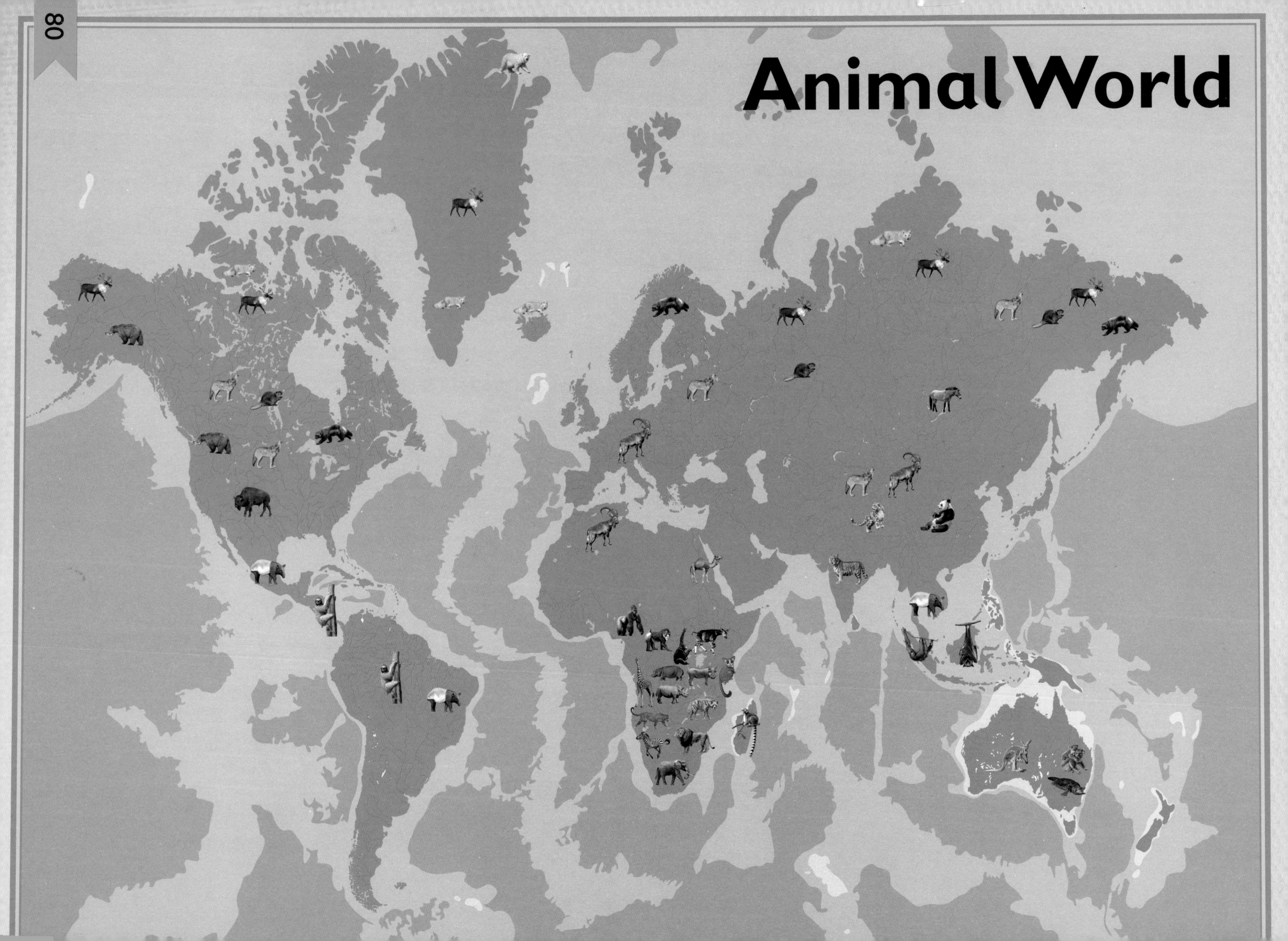
Animal World